Thomas Donnelly
Exhibition Catalogue

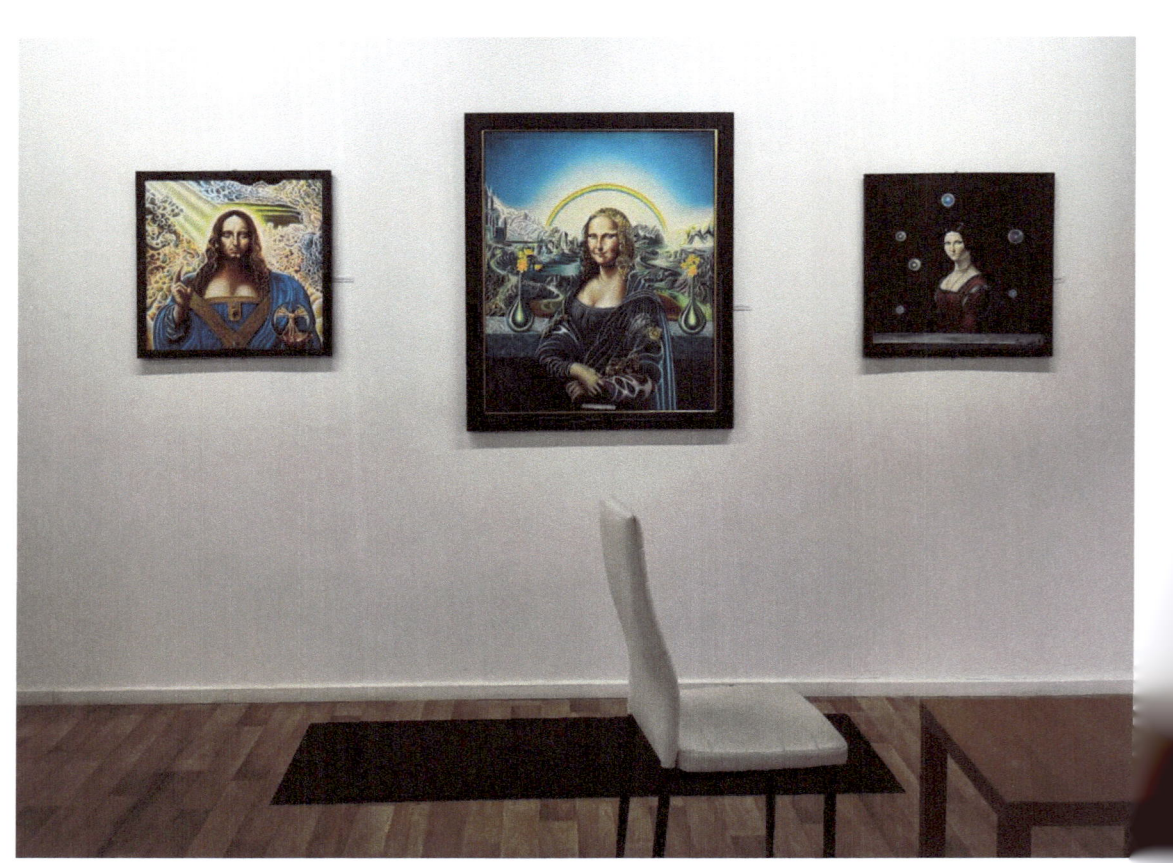

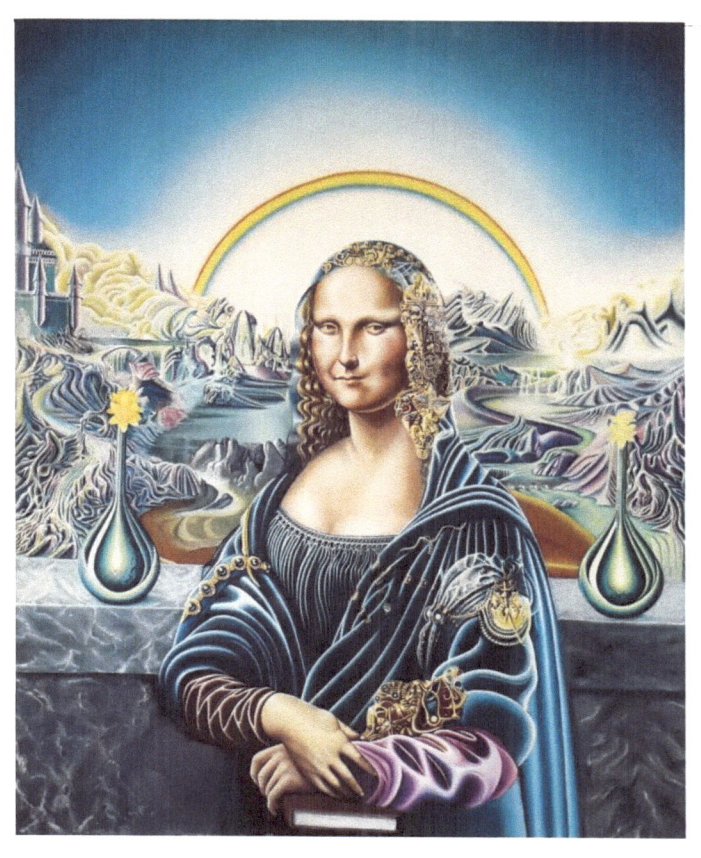

Thomas Donnelly
Paintings
July 1 - 29 2023

Studio and Gallery
Main Street, Kilbirnie

Studio and Gallery
2 Craighouse Square
Kilbirnie
KA25 7AF
U.K.

www.alchemywebsite.com

Thomas Donnelly began painting around 2010. He was taken with the paintings of Leonardo da Vinci and felt he wanted to try and paint a copy of the well known work, the *Mona Lisa*. Not having any artistic training, it took him some years to solve the problems of creating an oil painting. As he worked on the piece he kept adding more and more decorative elements until the work became delightfully complex. During its creation few people saw the piece, and unfortunately Thomas got little encouragement, but his strong will and desire to see it finished prevailed.

In 2017 I set up my art gallery in Kilbirnie. As I was looking for local artists to exhibit, news reached me that an artist here in Kilbirnie had created a version of the *Mona Lisa*. I initially dismissed this, as so many people have created rather poor copies of this painting.

Later that year, Thomas turned up in my gallery, pulled out his phone and wanted to show me his painting. This is something that must happen all the time to gallery owners. I glanced at the poor quality photograph, expecting to have to find some way of dismissing him without being too brutal. As I looked at the two inch high photograph on his phone, I could see it clearly had considerable merit. I asked Thomas if I could come to his house and view it. He said there was no need for that. He would bring it down to the gallery, as he lived only a few hunded yards away. A few minutes later he appeared bearing the large painting.

I was immediately shocked and amazed at the elaborate detail with which Thomas had embellished the work. I immediately began to appraise and analyse his work, pointing out how much I admired his technique and composition. I suspect this was the first time that Thomas had received a positive response to his art. I immediately offered him an exhibition in my gallery, but was dismayed when he said this was his only work and it was still unfinished.

Thomas had begun this painting seven years earlier in 2010, but due to pressures of life had then abandoned it. My positive response made him decide to finish it, and even to consider working on other pieces.

Early in 2019, I was becoming aware of the growth of mural art, in Scotland, specially in Glasgow. I wondered if I could create a mural on the gable end of the gallery. I toyed with a number of ideas, but these did not seem suitable for the environment of the town of Kilbirnie. I suddenly realised that Thomas' *Mona Lisa* had the right proportions for the wall and that it would be most appropriate for the mural to have been created by a local artist. It took a few months to convince the local planning office to approve it, but we pushed on and in July 2019, the *Kilbirnie Mona Lisa* was installed.

By then Thomas had begun working on other paintings. His style drew from the Old Masters but his reworking required hundreds of hours of meticulous work using the finest of paint brushes, so it took another four years before Thomas had produced a body of work that could fill the gallery space. He experimented with some simple portraits, but he was always drawn to the style shaped by his work on the Mona Lisa. When the *Salvator Mundi*, attributed to Leonardo, was promoted in the media in 2017-18, I wasn't at all surprised that Thomas would be inspired to make a painting based on this theme.

Recently, he has aquainted himself with many 16th and 17th century paintings as he is drawn to that style and quality of painting. Each of his works takes hundreds of hours od intense work, so they are necessarly expensive purchases. He models each element, so his paintings are never flat but the forms stand out three-dimensionally. His figures engage, even challenge the viewer.

The Kilbirnie Mona Lisa Mural

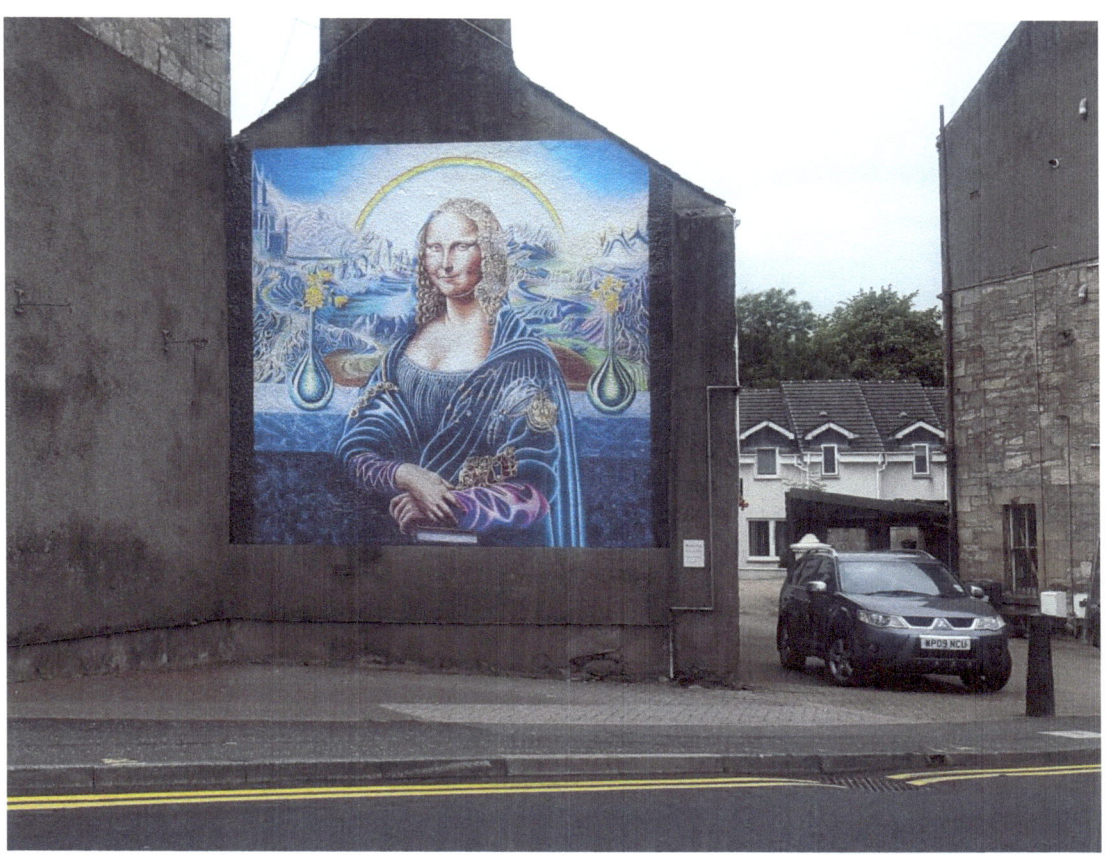

The Kilbirnie Mona Lisa painting (100x80 cm)

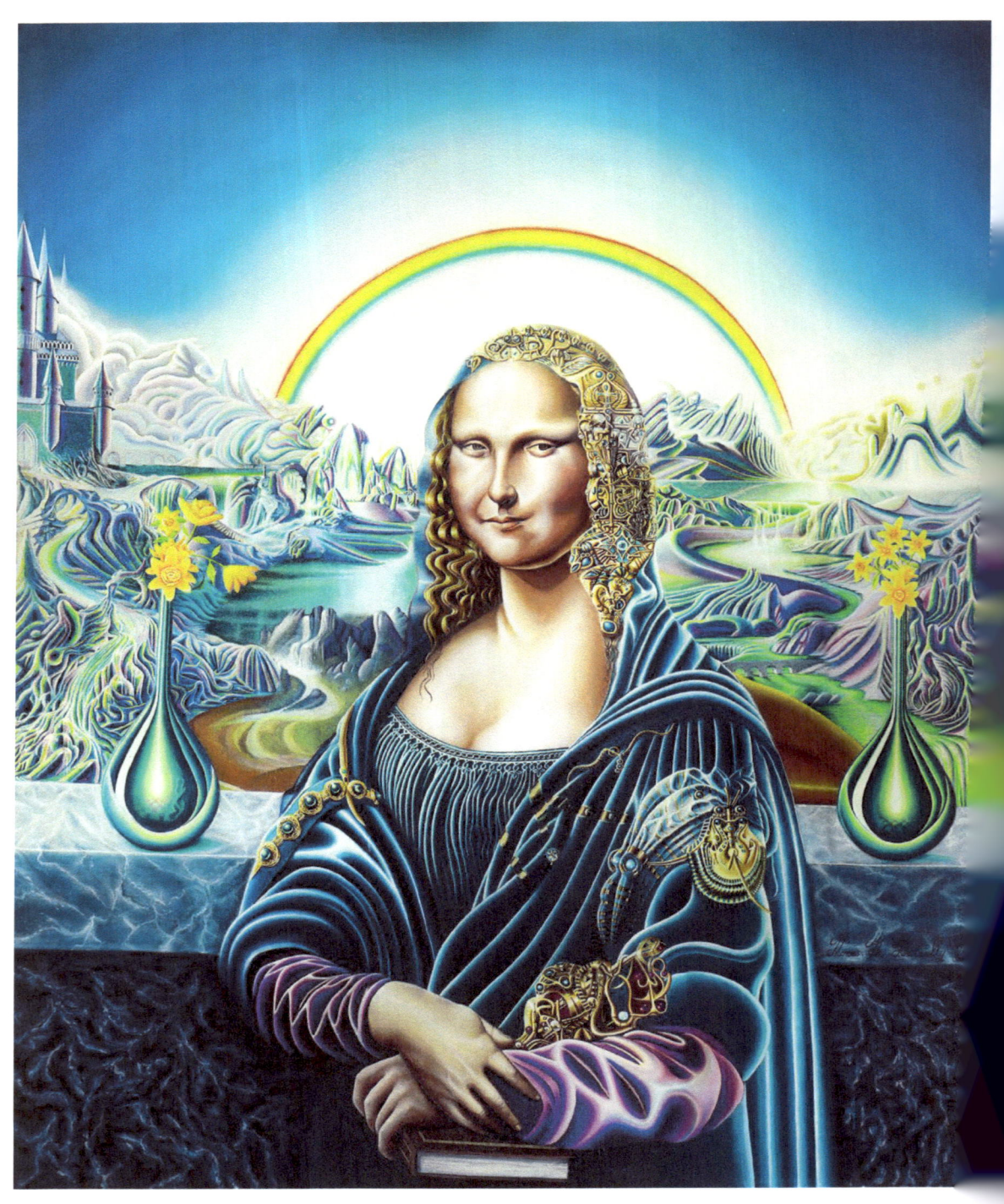

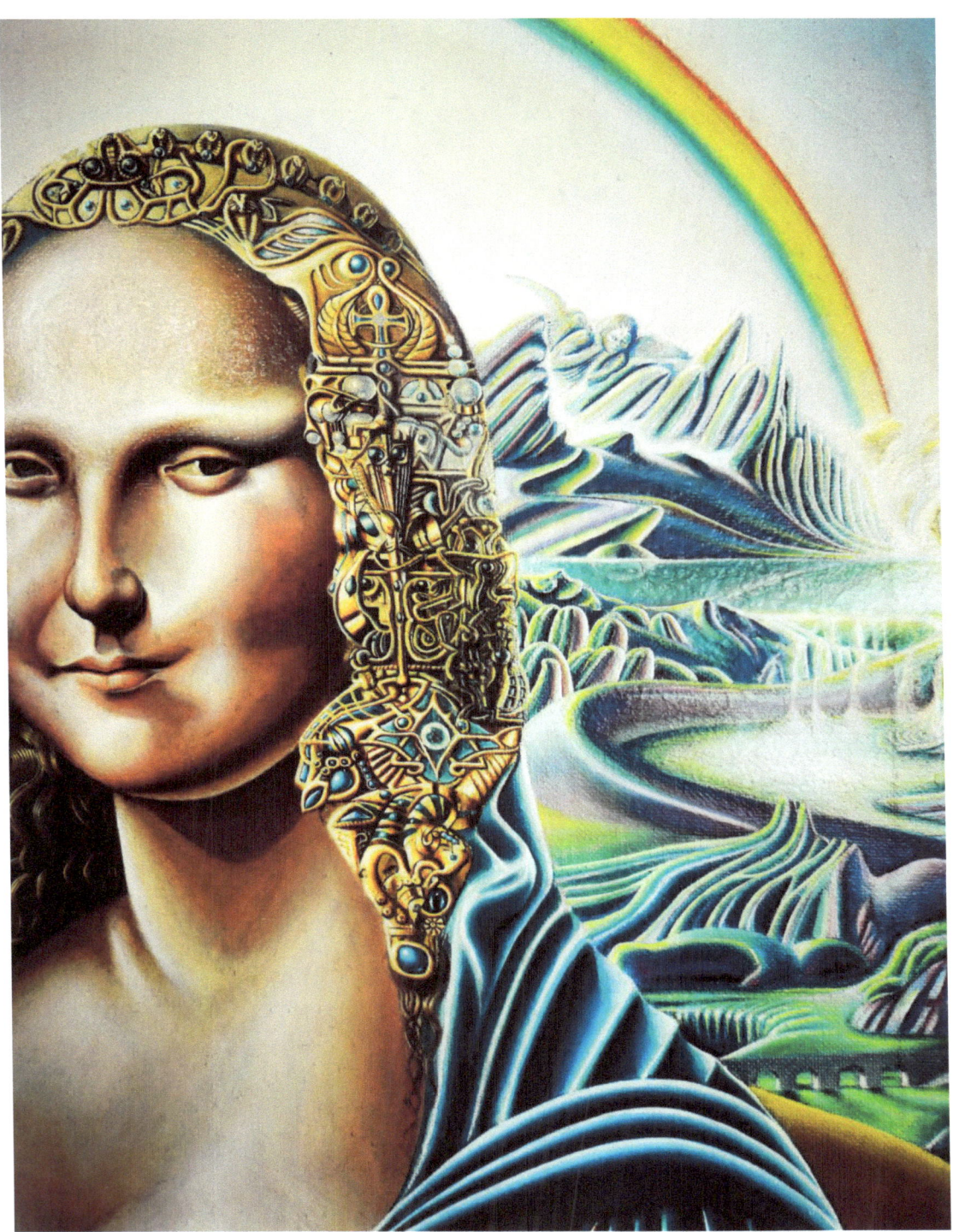

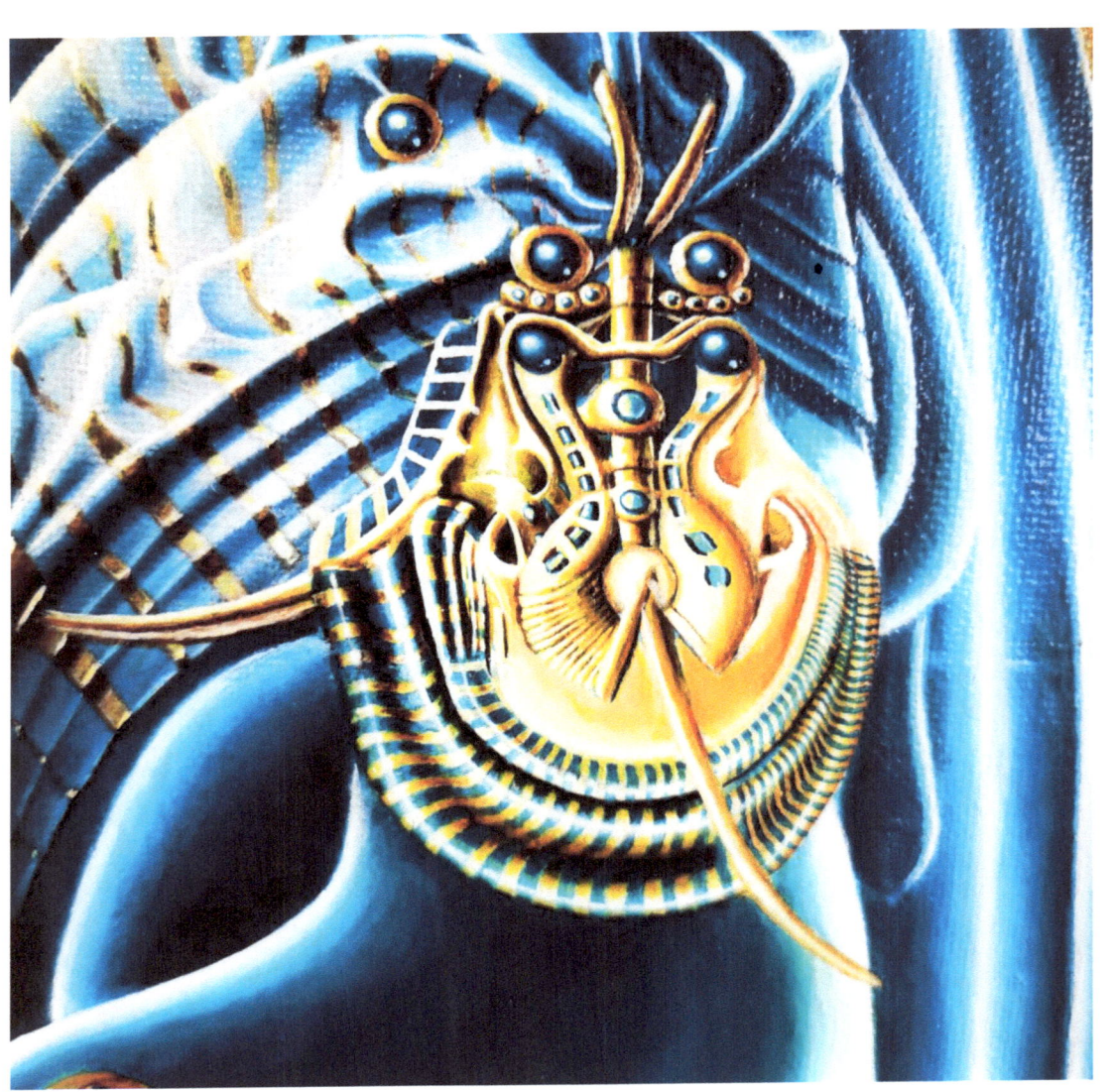

Present Gaze (40x58 cm)

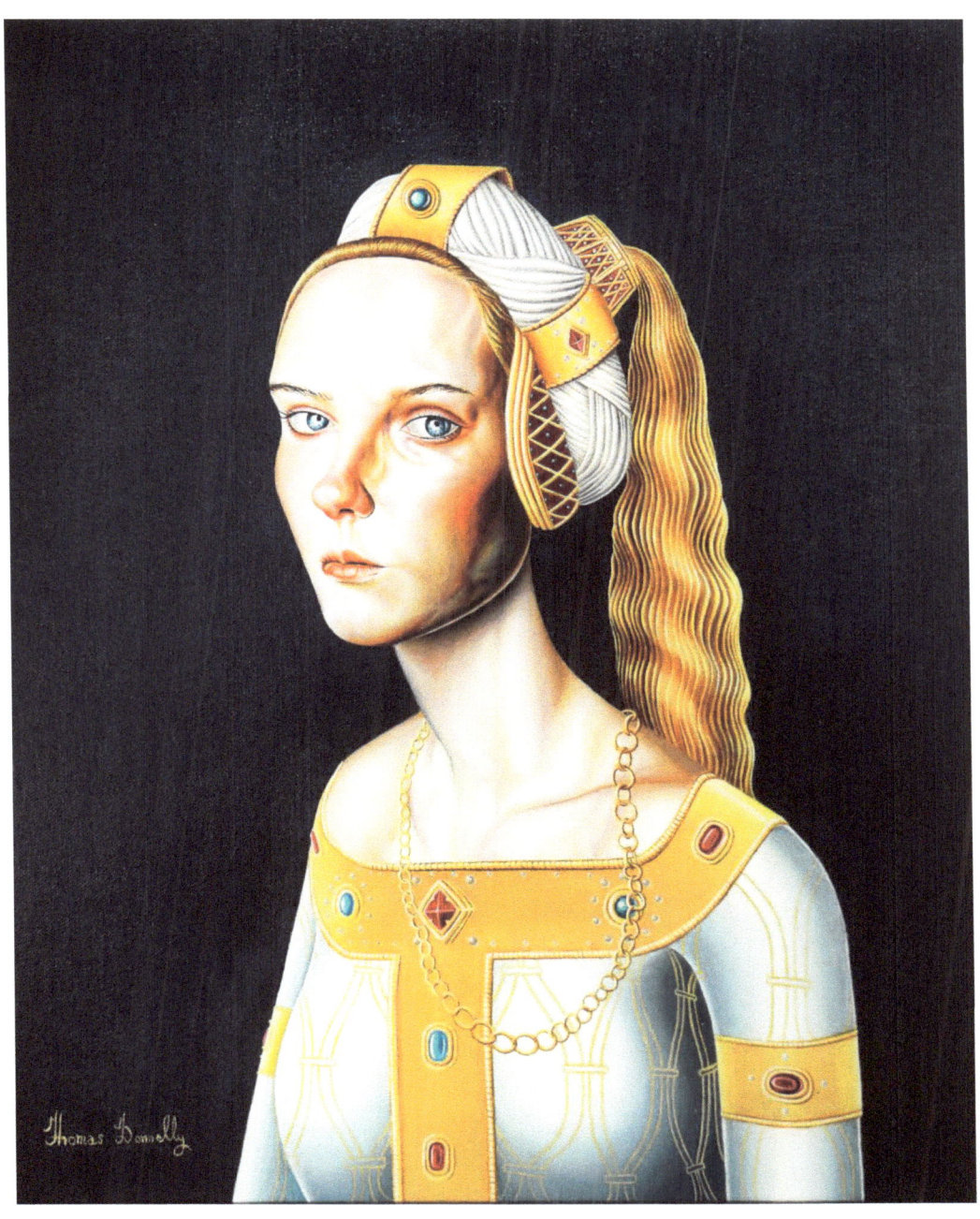

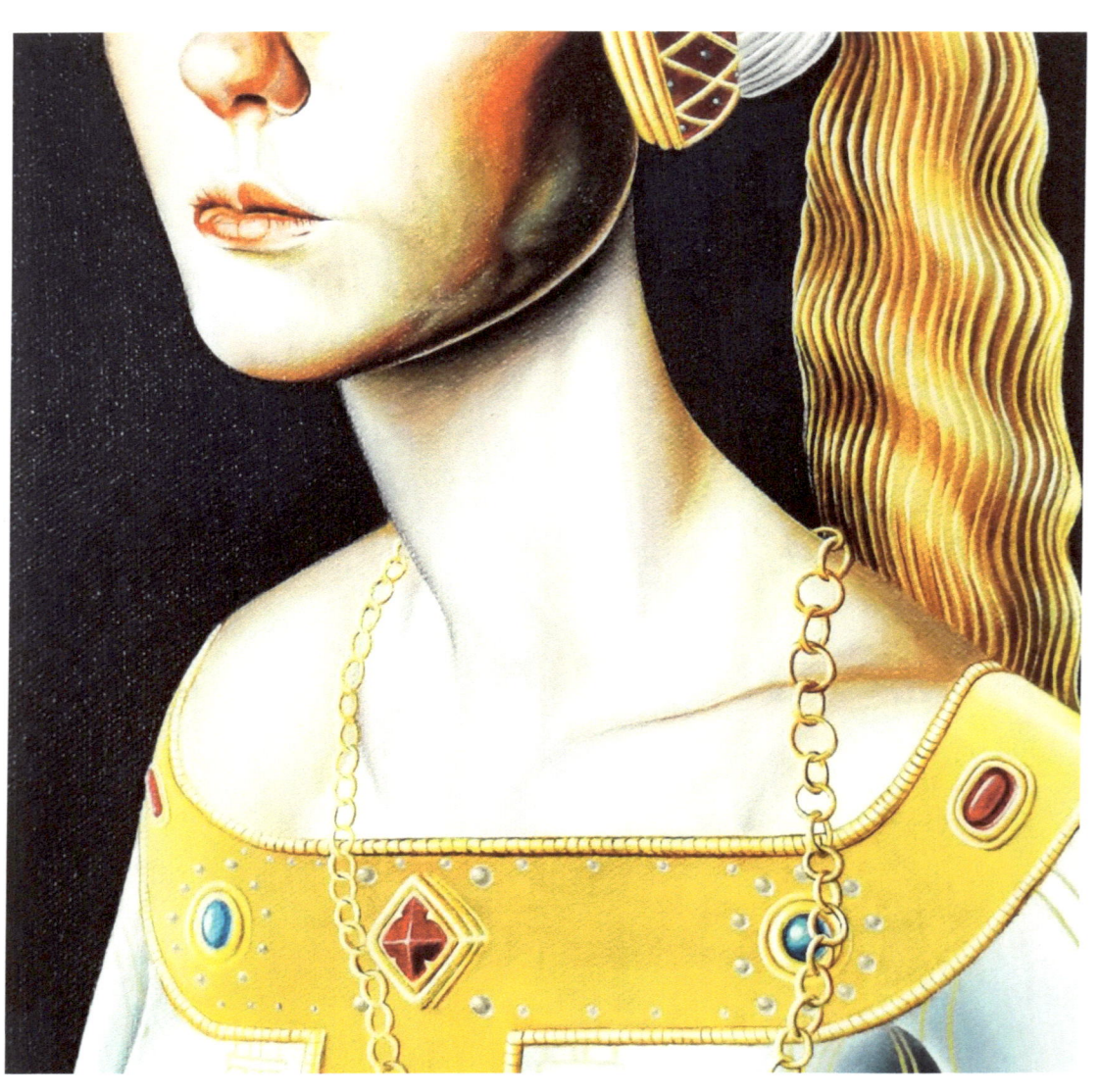

Adornment (51x61 cm)

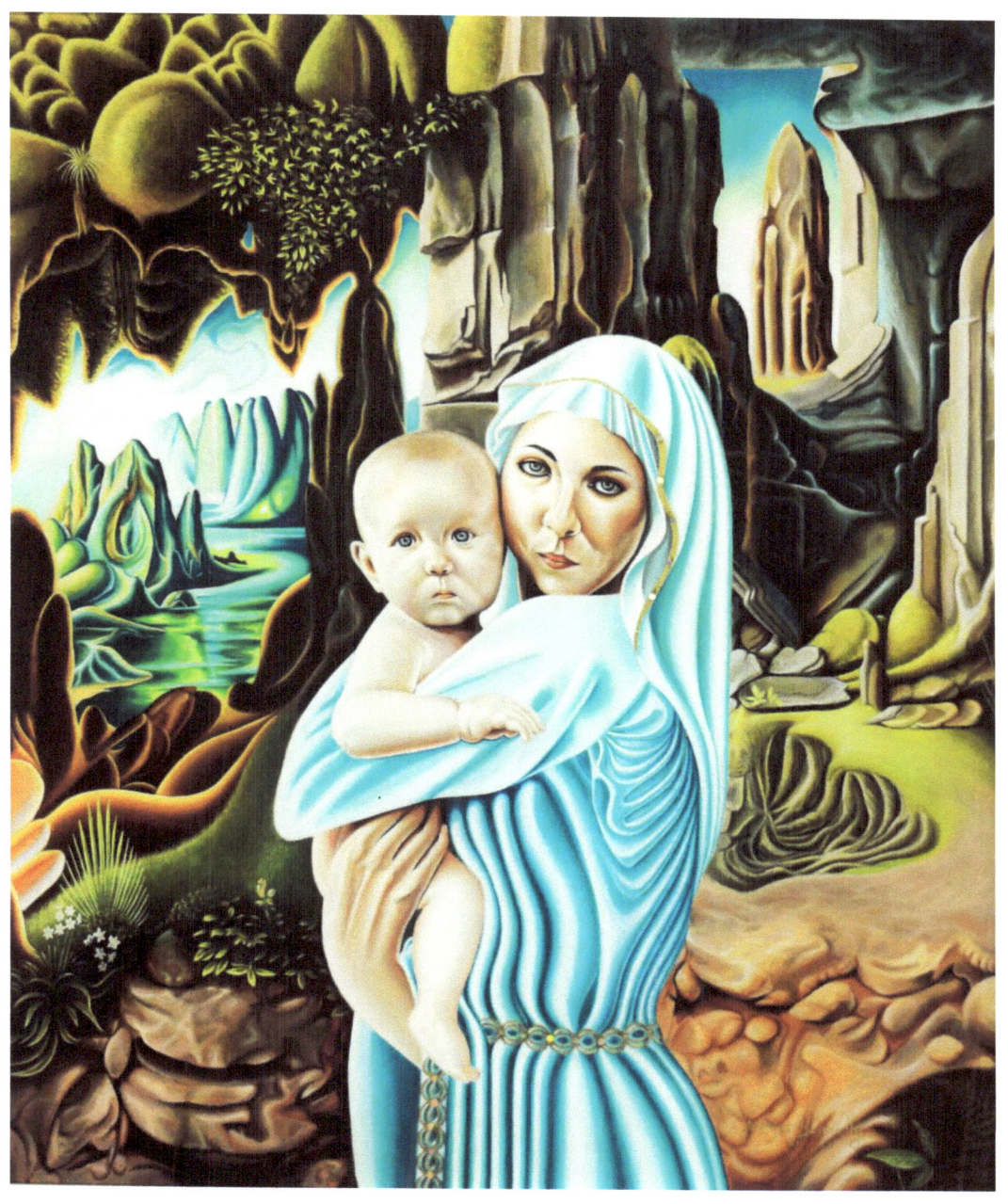

Phos, the Bringer of Light (61x61cm)

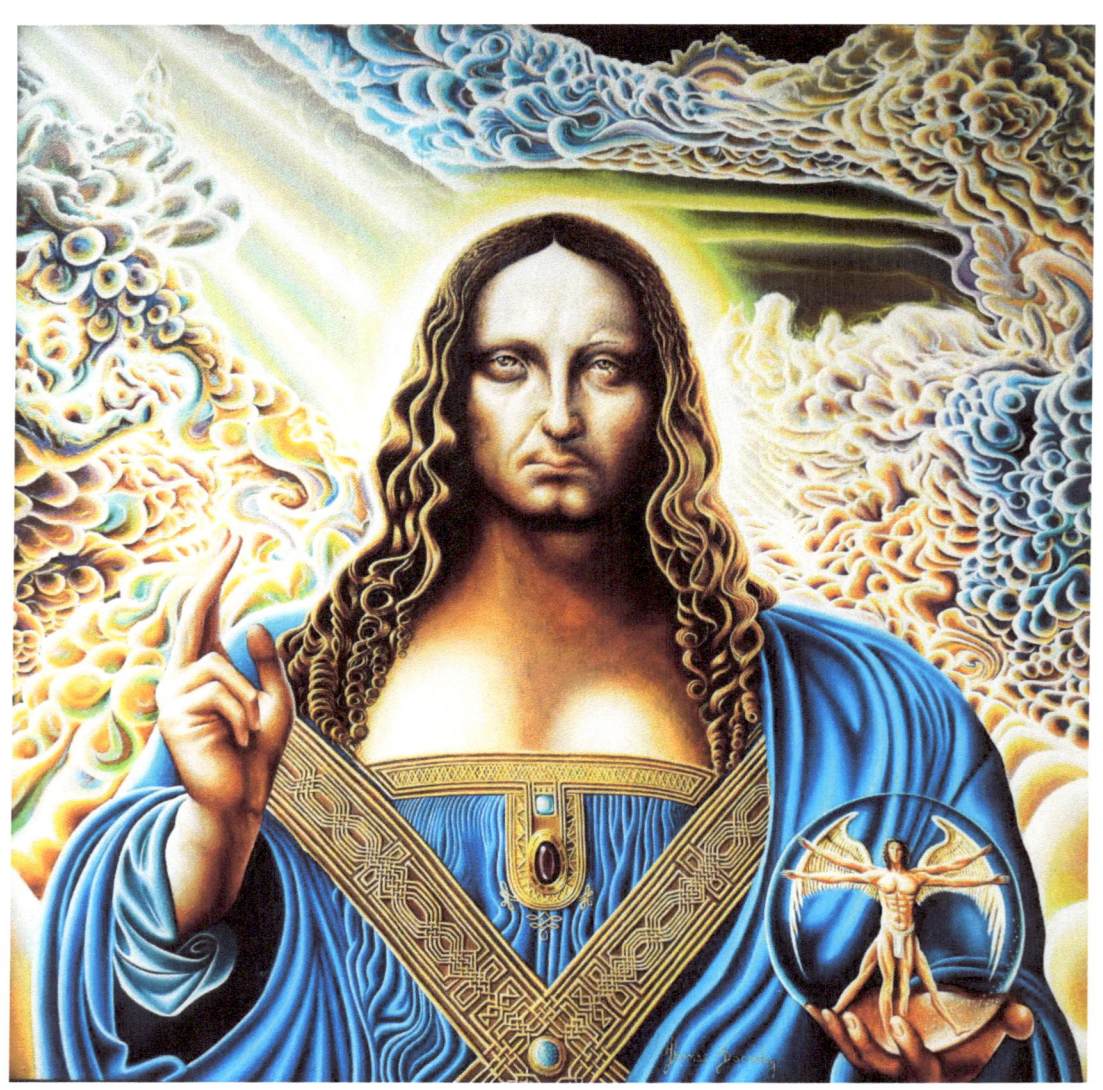

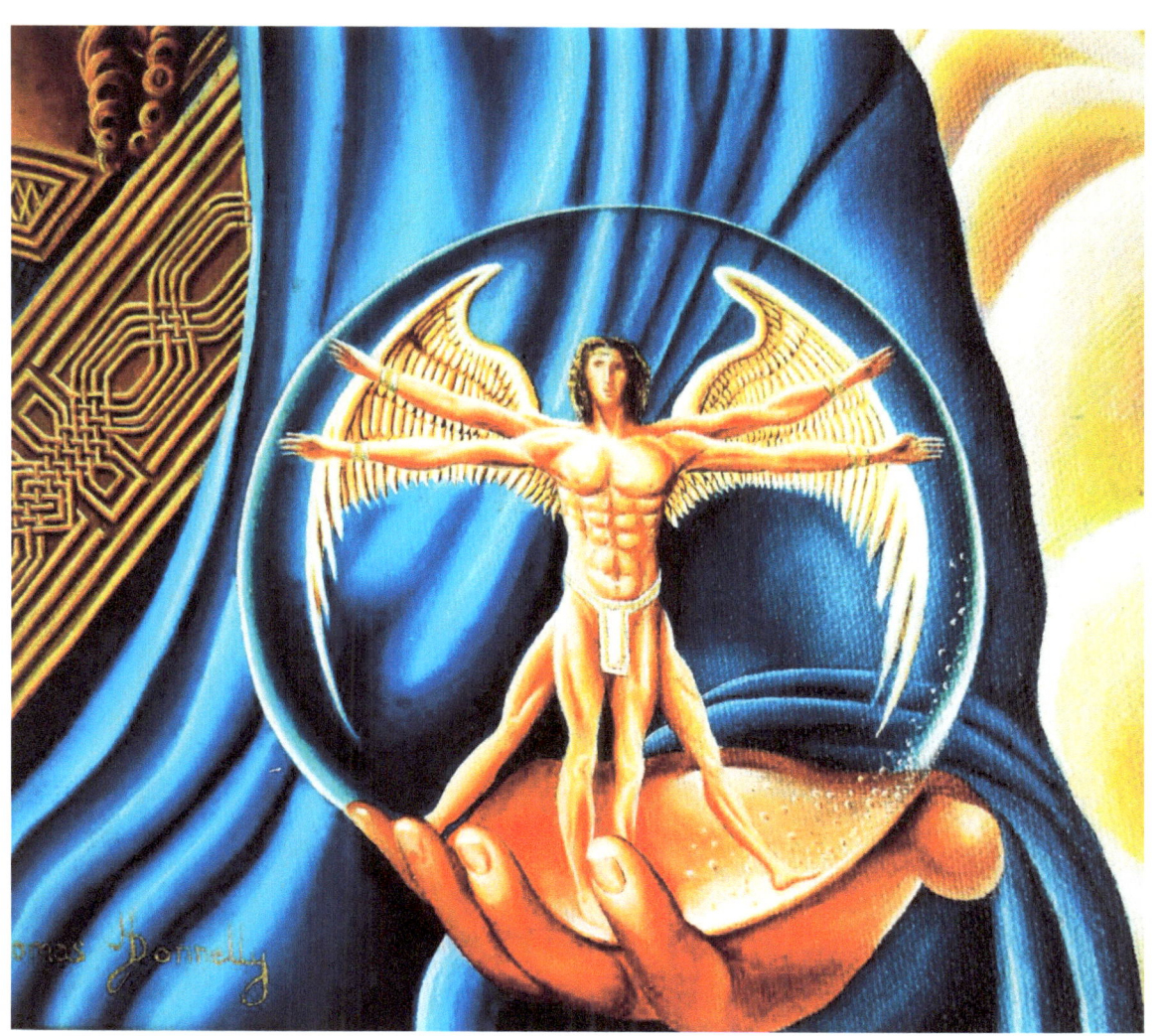

Seraphim's Sword (50x40 cm)

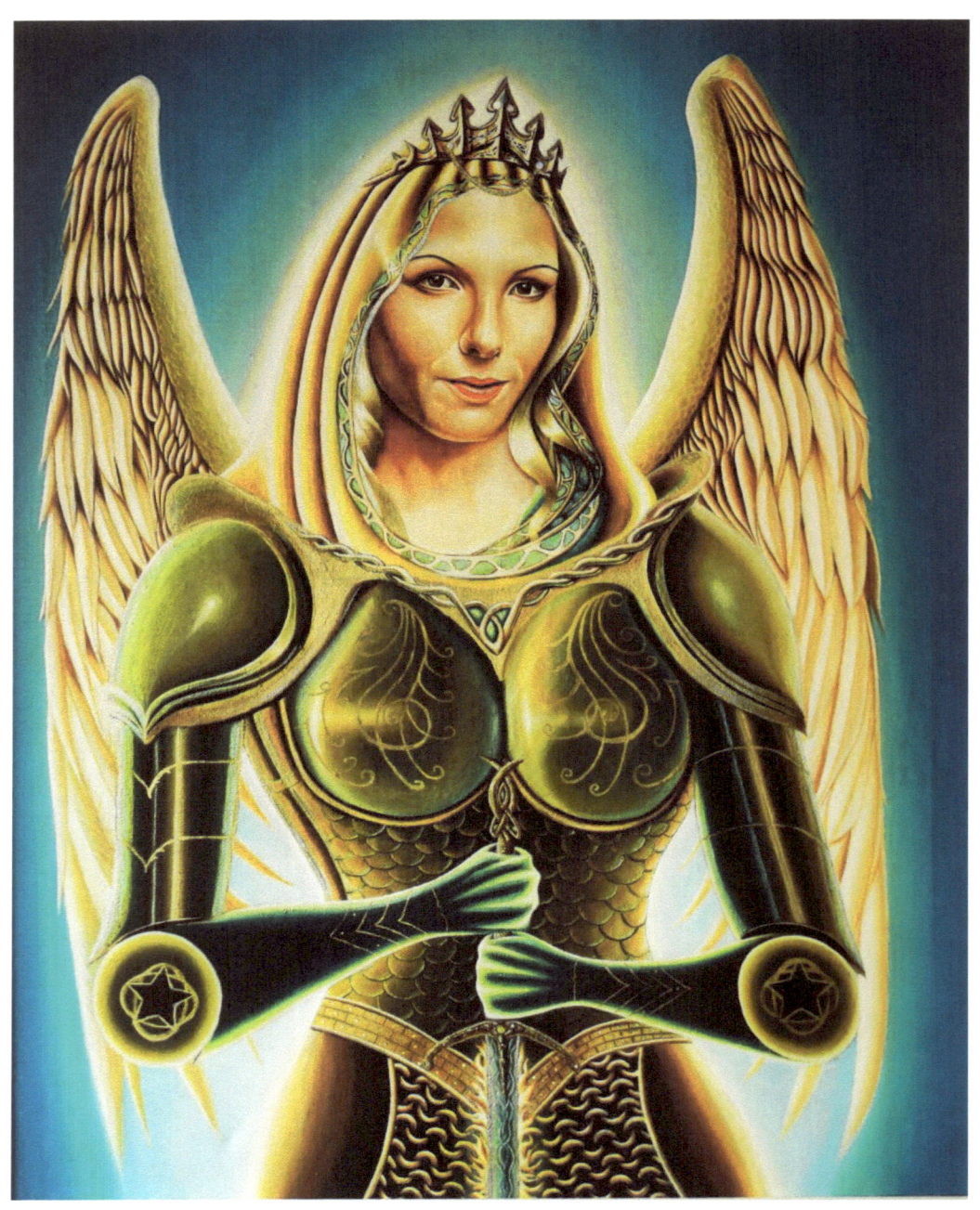

Cupid's Bow (50x40 cm)

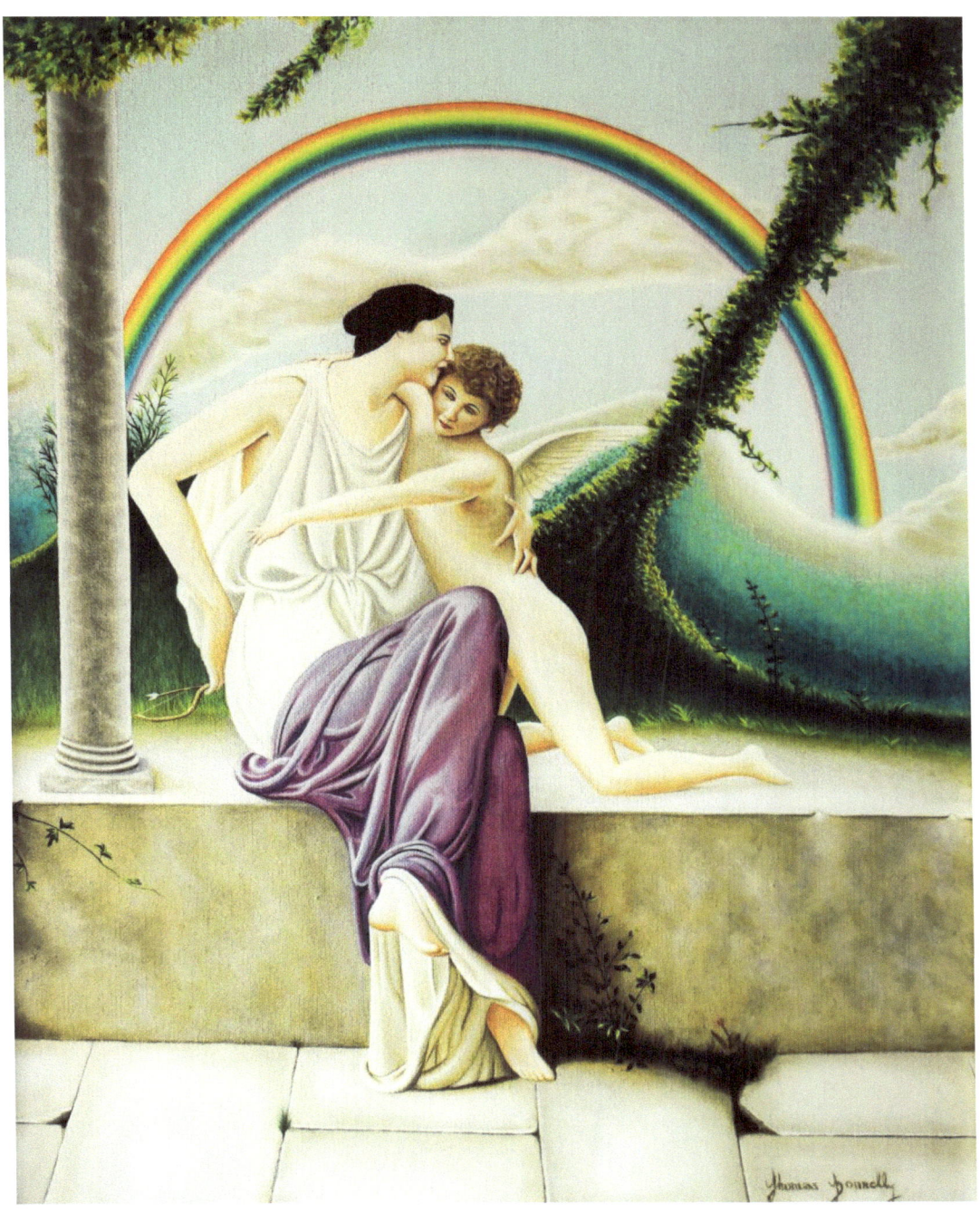

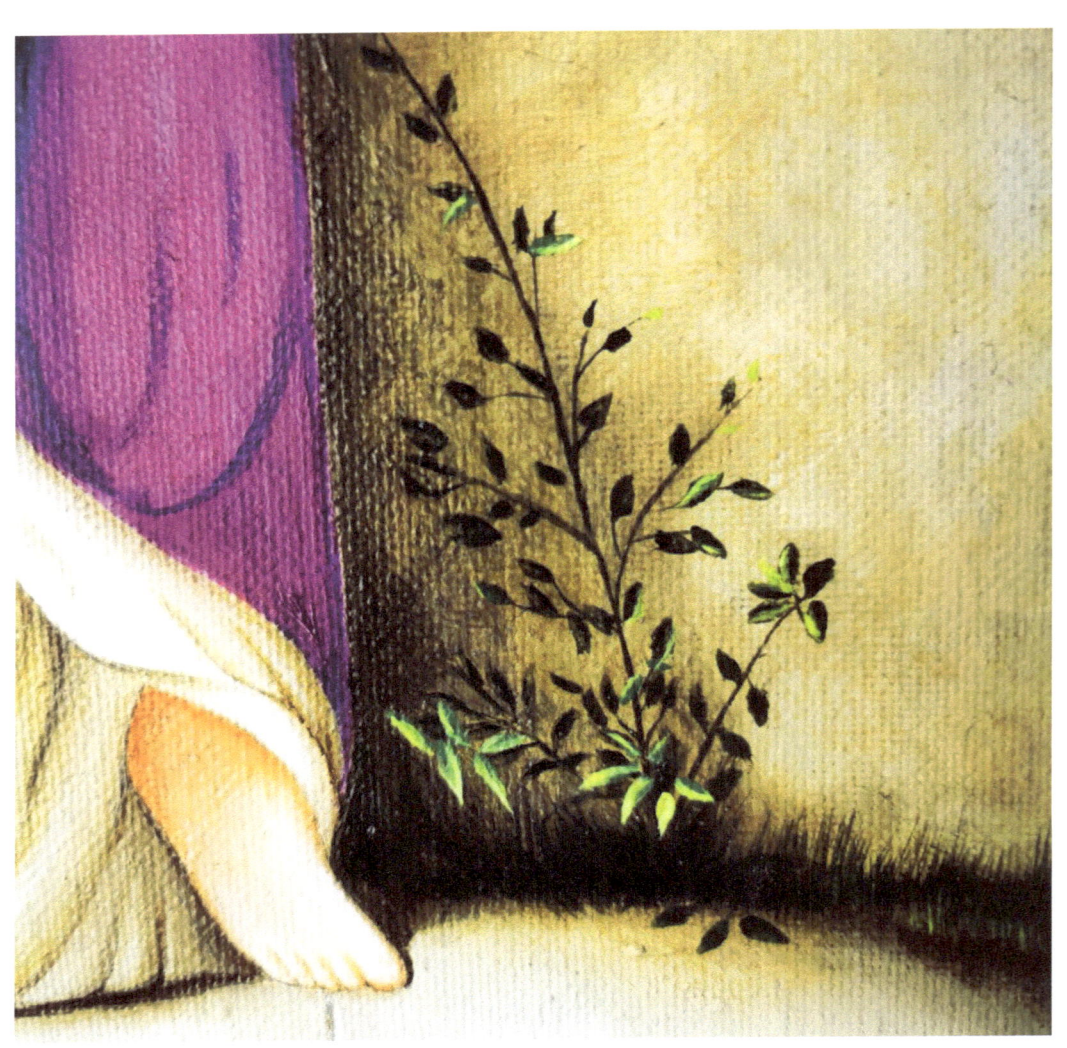

Gaia's Grief (50x40 cm)

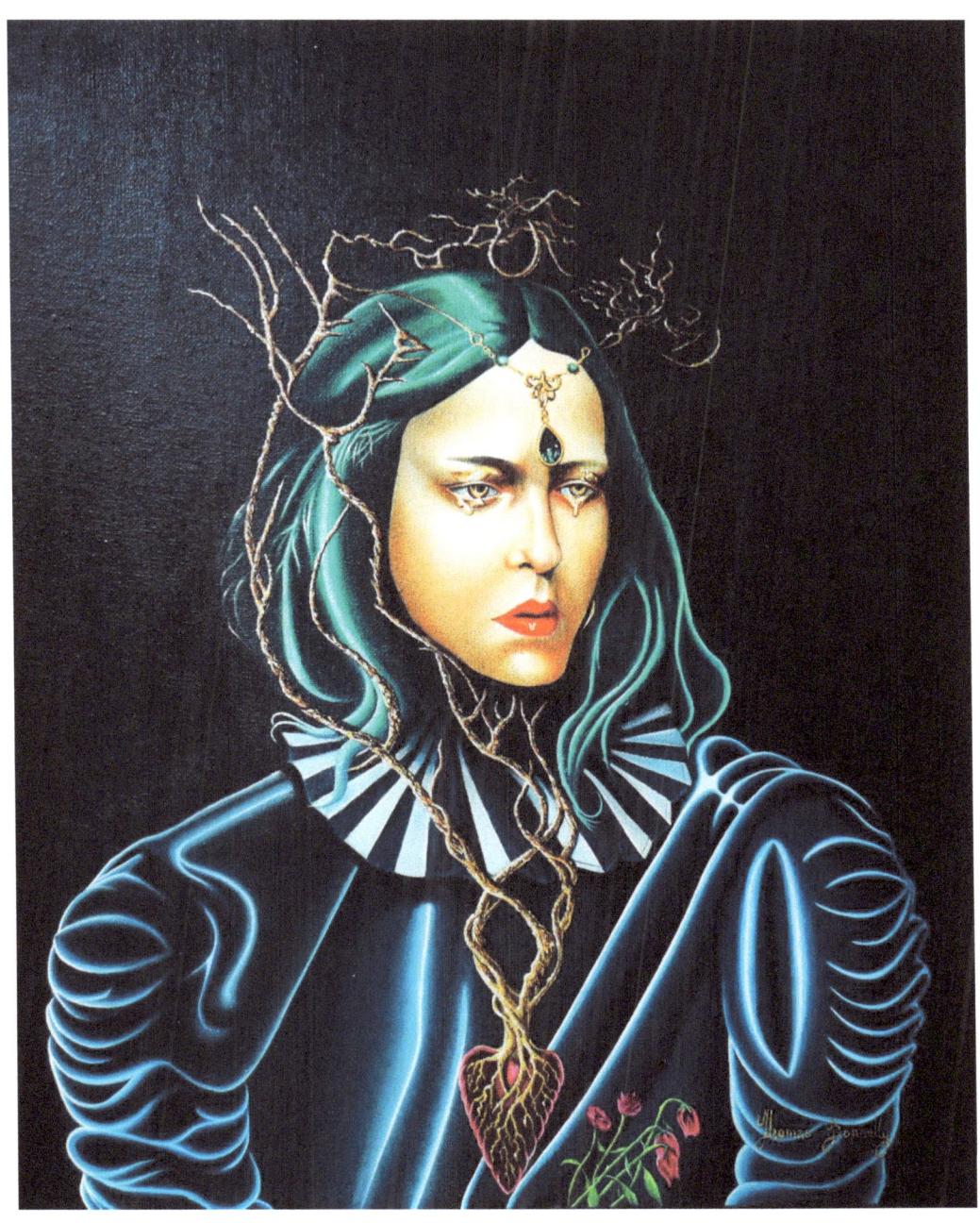

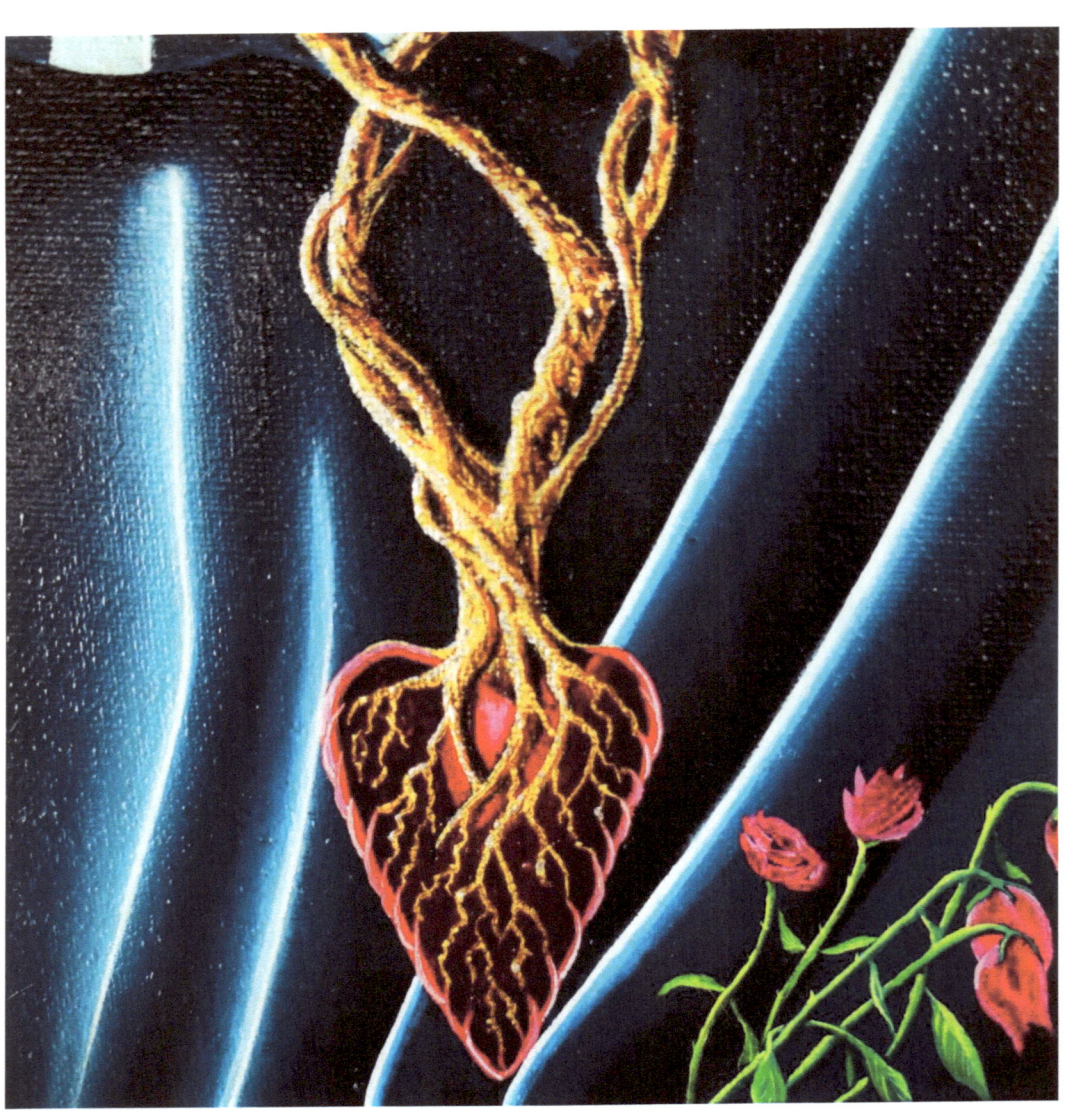

Cogitatio of the Soul (36x28 cm)

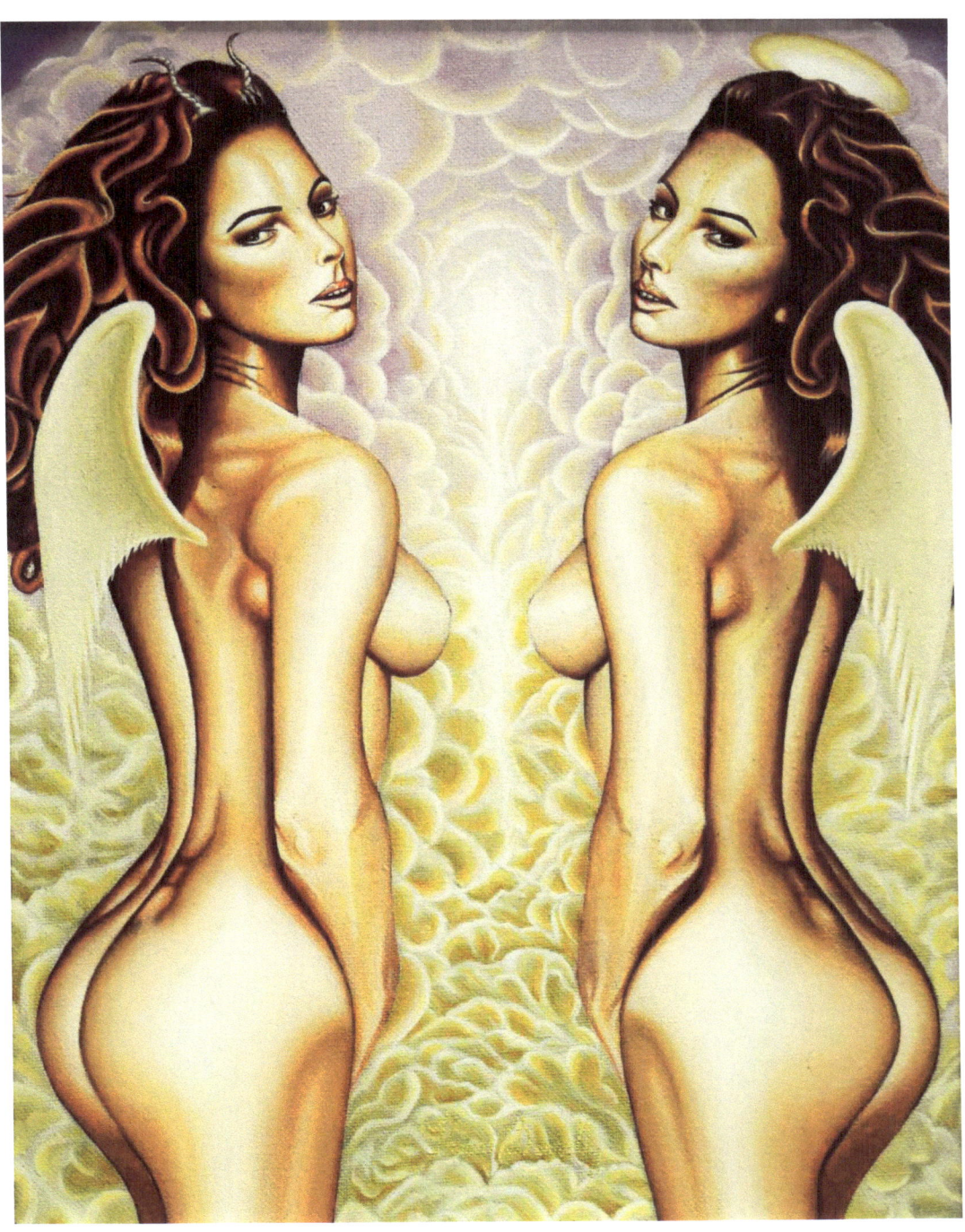

Sorrowful soul (41x58 cm)

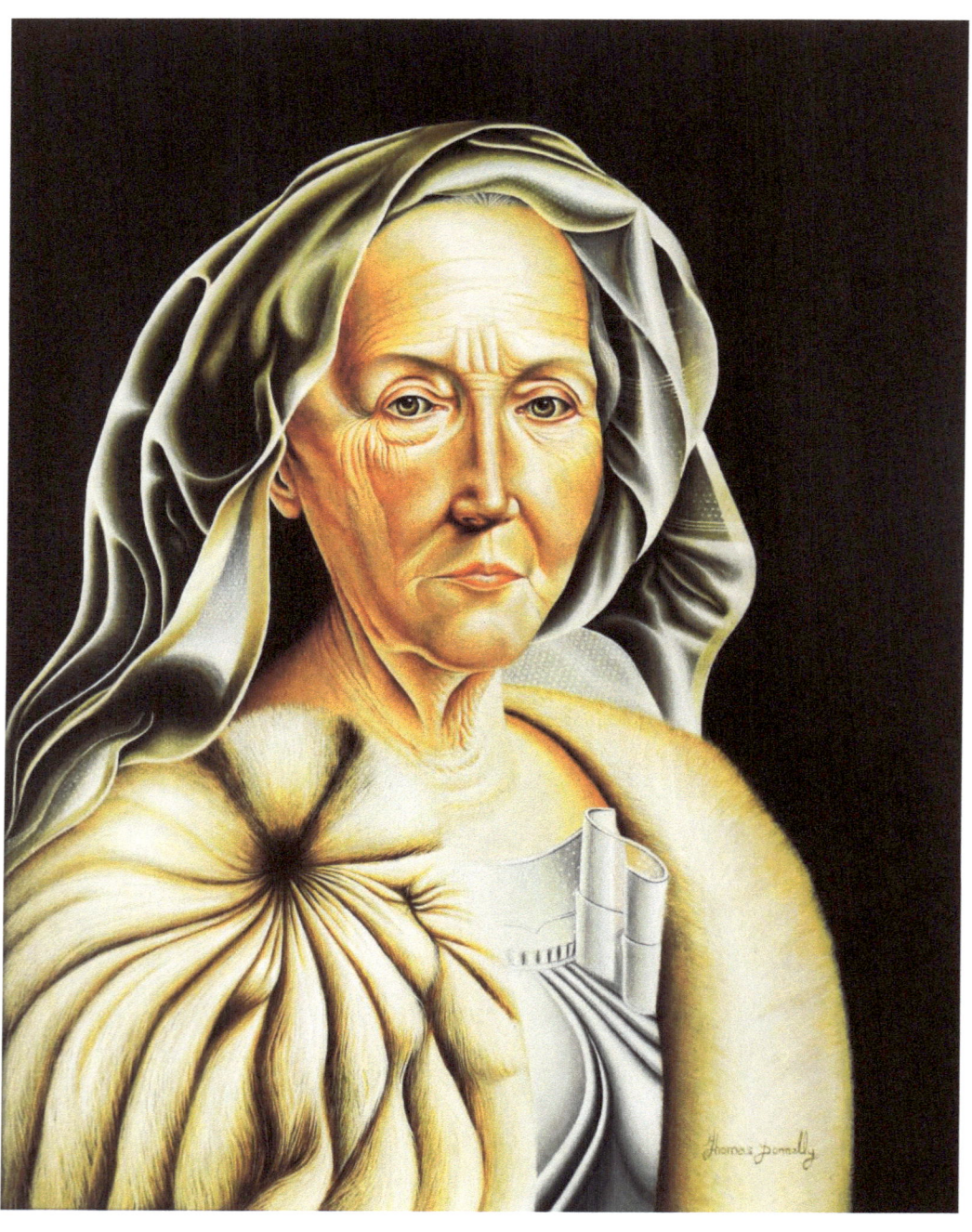

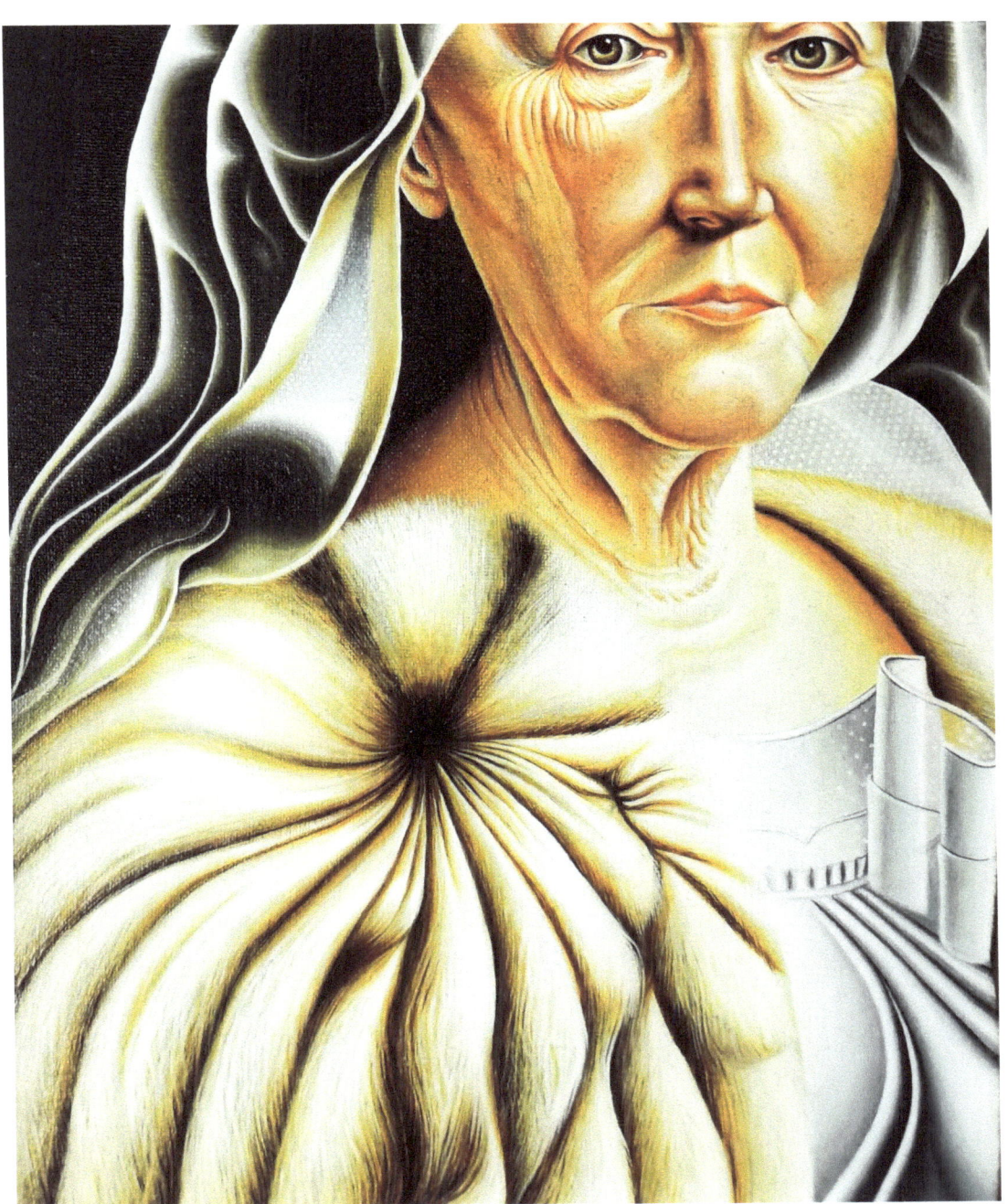

As above, so below (41x58 cm)

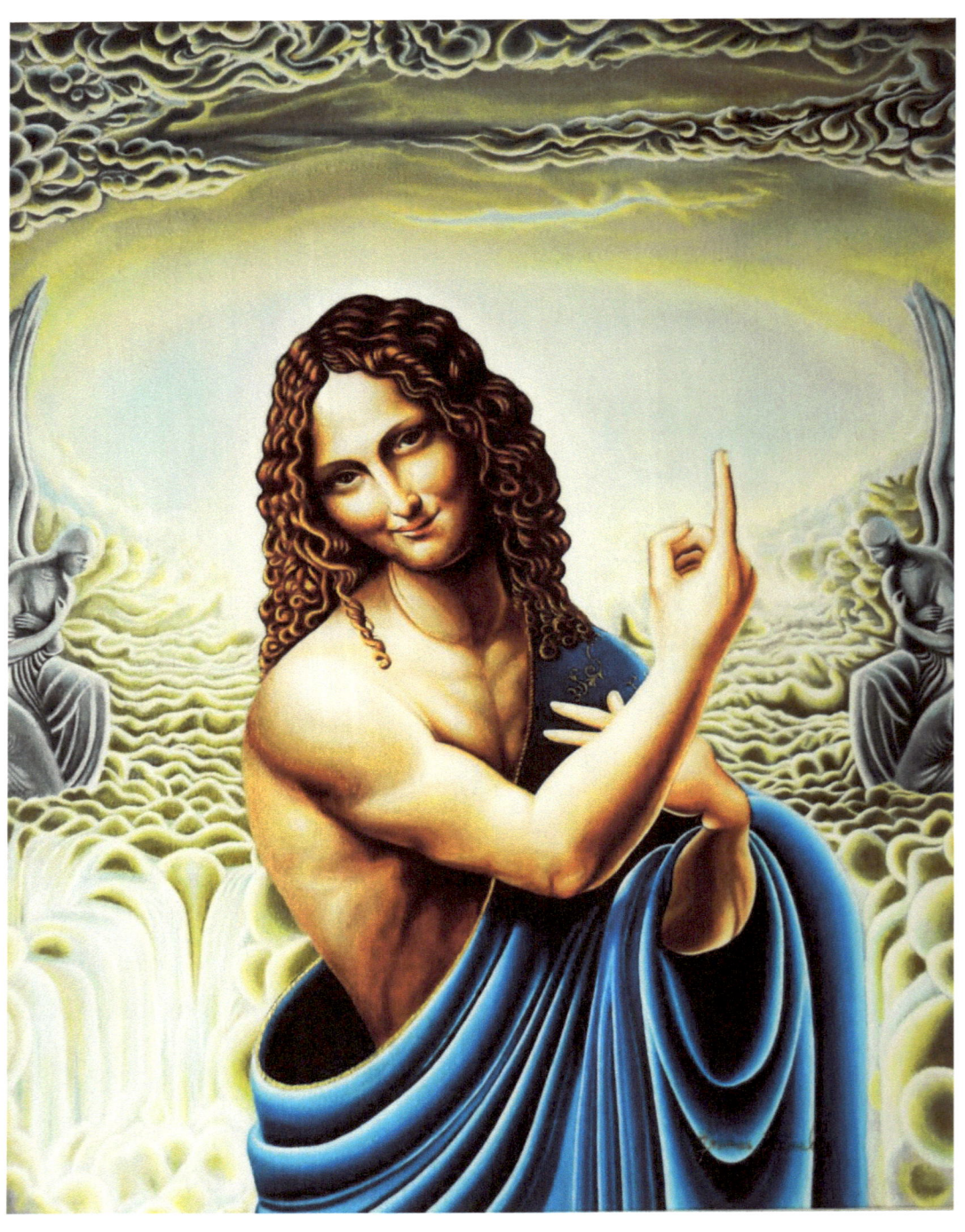

La belle Ferronnière (61x61 cm)

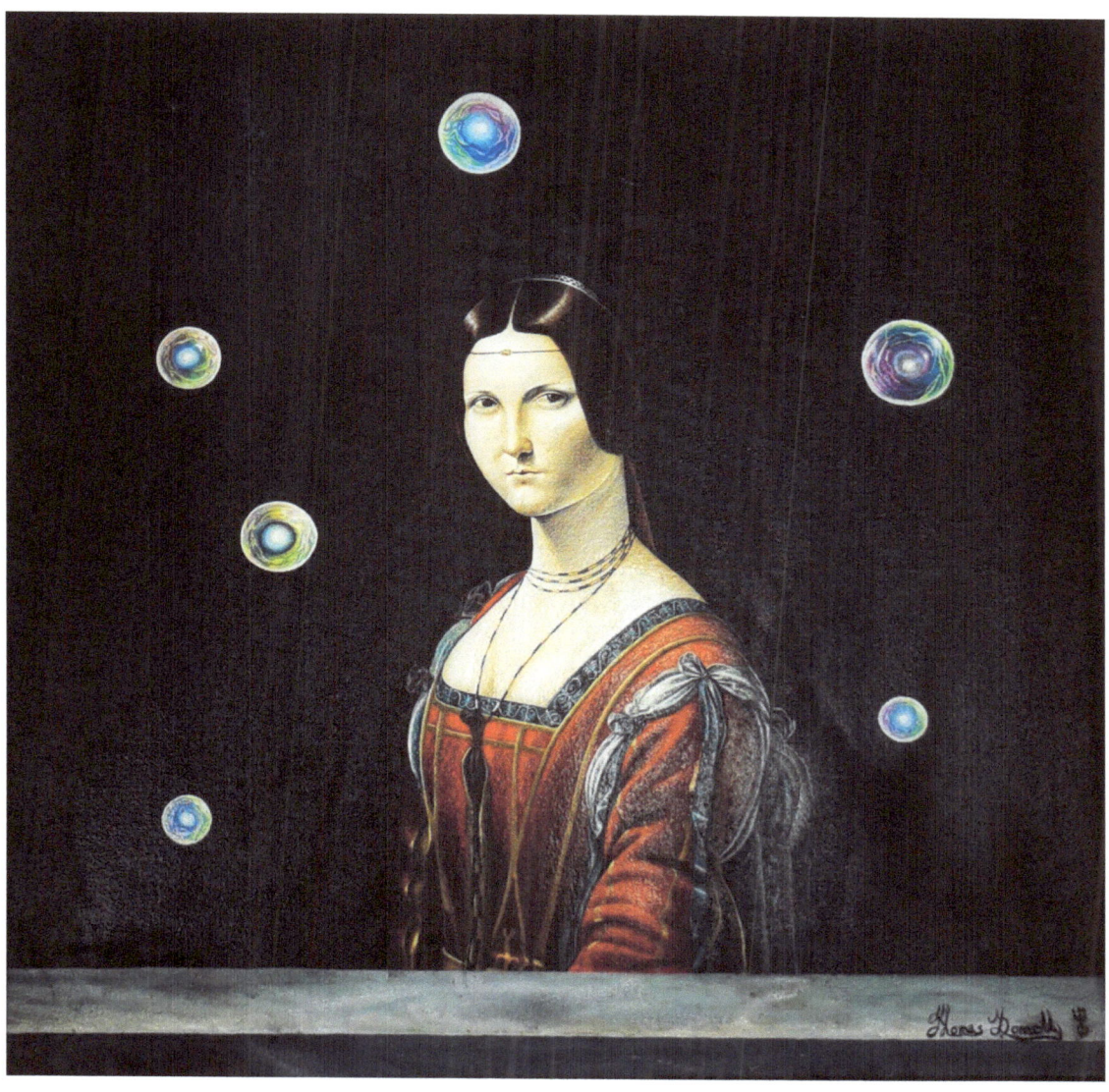

The Student (41x30 cm)

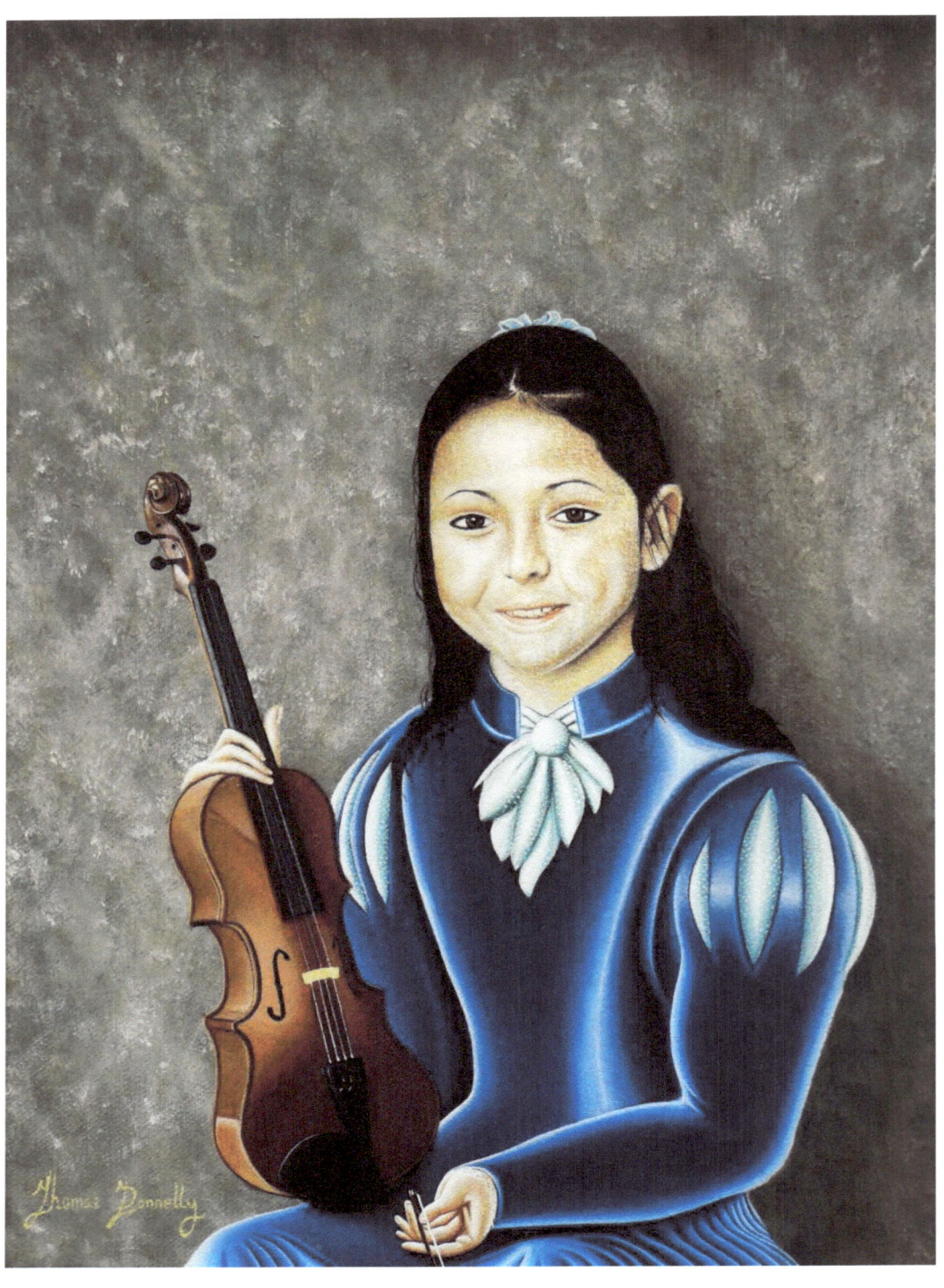

Girl with the pearl earing (31x25 cm)

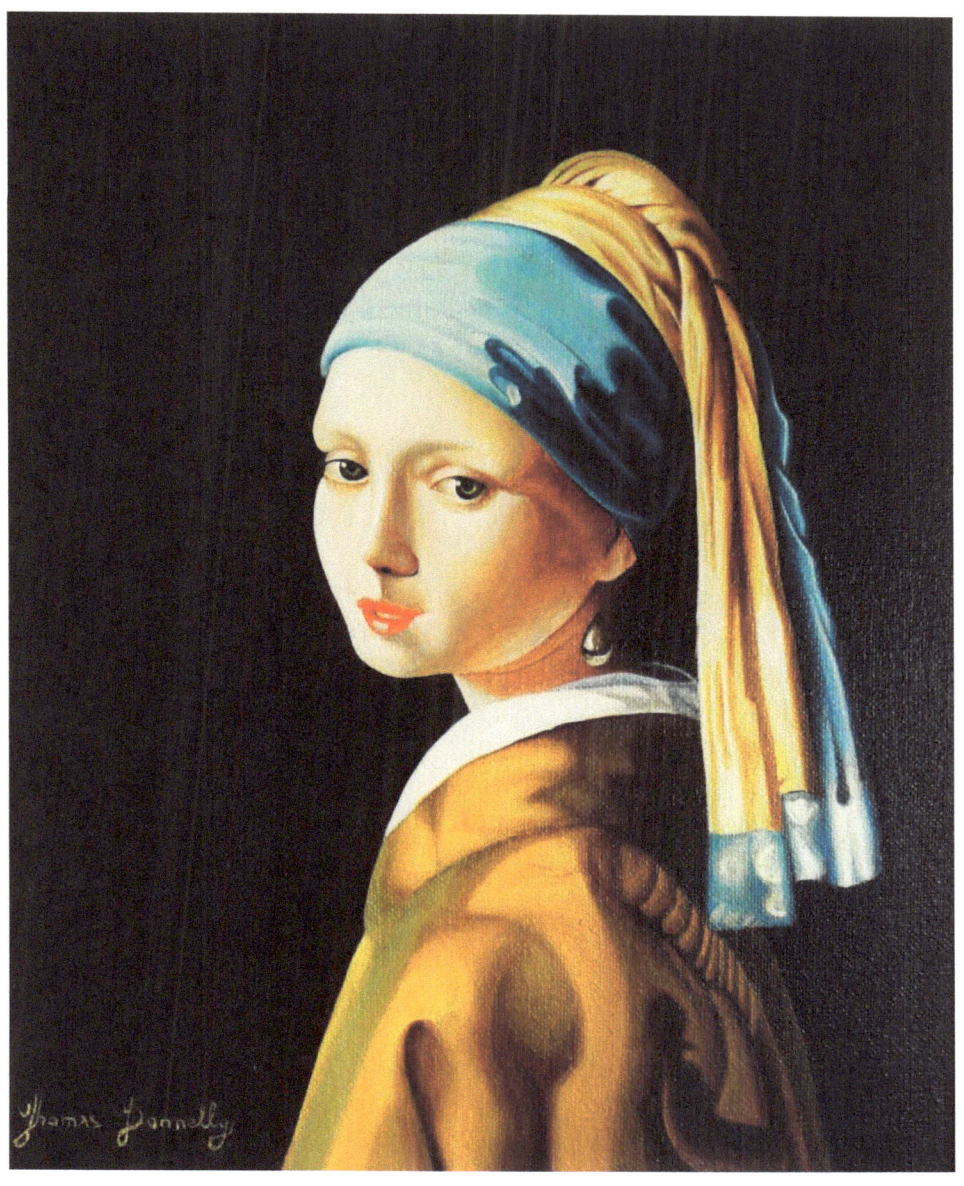

Bowie the White Duke (41x58 cm)

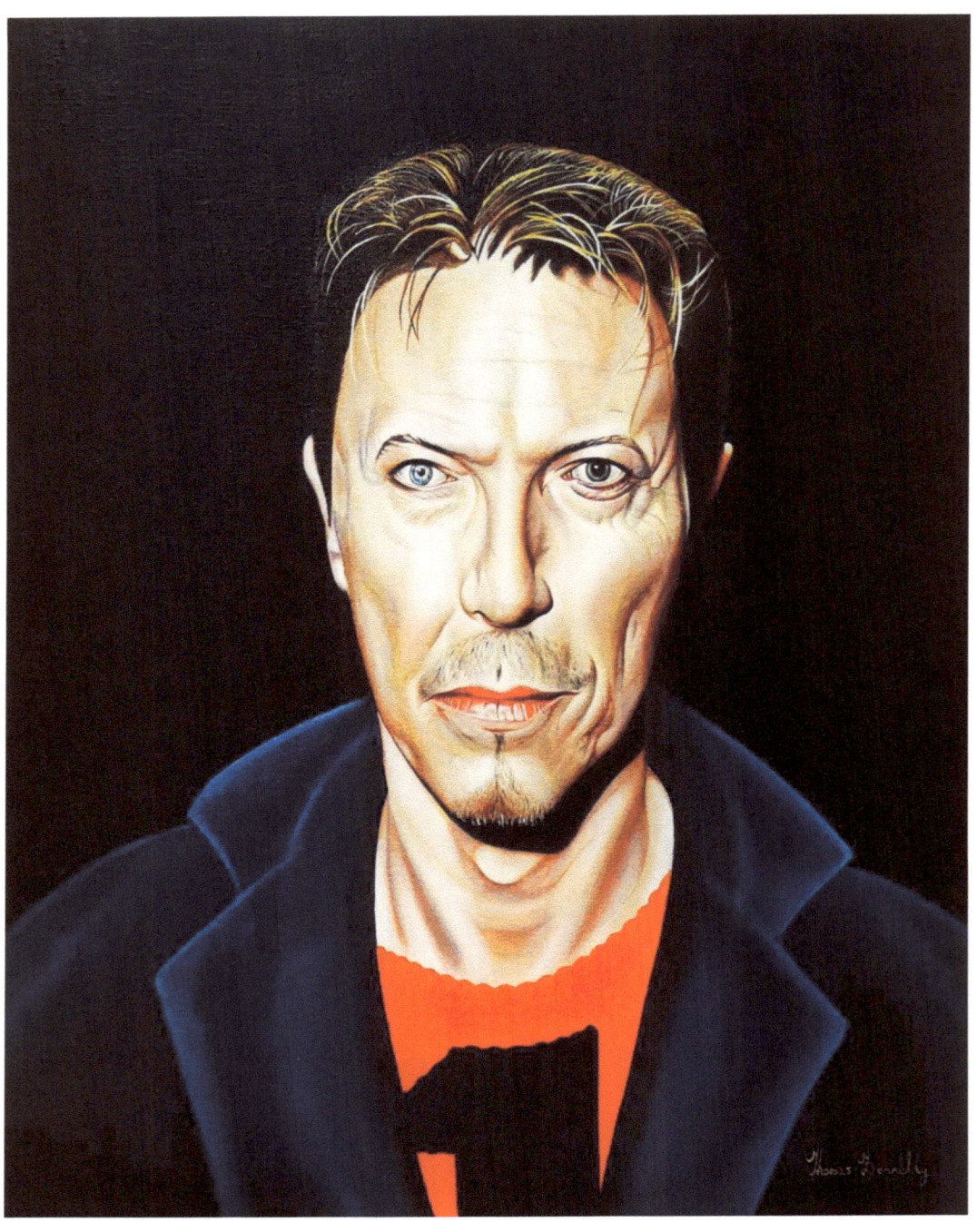